Contents

90

Equal grouping

Count the orange flowers. Now count the blue vases.
The flowers must be grouped equally into each vase.
How many flowers should be in each of
the blue vases?

Now look at the other flowers and vases.
How many flowers should be grouped
equally in each vase?

5

Equal sharing

Count the bones. Then count the dogs. Finally, share the bones equally between the dogs. Each dog must have the same number of bones.

Try this again with the other animals and things to share.

Challenge

You will need 20 counters, paper and a pencil. Draw 2 large circles. Can you share the 20 counters evenly between the 2 circles? Now try again for 3, 4, 5 and 10 circles. Which number of circles leaves some counters left over?

Dividing by 2

You can use what you know about multiplying by 2 to help you to divide by 2, so 5x2=10 then 10÷2=5.

How many cakes will fit into each box?

Now try this

Write out all the multiplication facts for the 2 times-table like this: 1x2=2 2x2=4.
Now write out the division facts for 2 like this: 2÷2=1 4÷2=2. Compare your 2 lists. What do you notice?

1x2=2
2x2=4
3x2=6

2÷2=1
4÷2=2
6÷2=3

9

Dividing by 10

Do this with a friend. You will each need some counters. Take turns to throw a counter onto the runway. Divide the number that your counter lands on by 10. Find the correct answer on the trucks and put a counter on it. The winner is the one with more counters on the trucks, when all 10 numbers are covered.

10   20   30

60   70   80

Use what you know about multiplying by 10 to help you to divide by 10, so 5x10=50 and 50÷10=5.

With a friend

Write down all the division facts for 10 in order: 10÷10=1 and so on. Now take turns to say a multiplication fact that goes with each division fact, such as 1 multiplied by 10 equals 10.

$$10 \div 10 = 1$$
$$1 \times 10 = 10$$

40   50

90   100

1 2 3 4 5

6 7 8 9 10

11

Dividing by 3, 4 and 5

Find out the number of each runner. Work out the answer to the division sentence on the runners' shirts. Find their missing number on the water bottles.

12÷3

20÷4

15÷5

10÷5

18÷3

24÷3

Which division sentences have an even answer?
Which division sentences have an odd answer?

Challenge

Some numbers can be divided by more than one number. For instance, 6 can be divided by both 2 and 3. Divide the numbers 12, 24, 36 by 3 and 4. What do you think will be the next number that can be divided by 3 and 4?

$12 \div 3 = 4$

$28 \div 4$

$45 \div 5$

$40 \div 4$

4

2

9

3

10

8

7

6

5

Finding remainders

Count the rabbits. Put the rabbits into the 2 hutches so that each hutch has the same number of rabbits. Sometimes when we divide, it is not possible to do this exactly. There is a remainder, or something left over. How many rabbits are left over?

Now try this with the other animals and their homes.
Find the remainders.

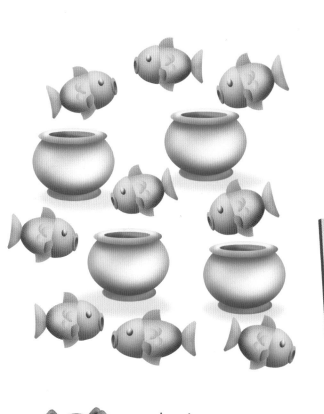

Challenge

Which numbers will divide into 30 without leaving a remainder?
Try dividing by 2, 3, 4, 5 and 10.

$$30 \div 2 =$$
$$30 \div 3 =$$
$$30 \div 4 =$$

15

Halves and quarters

Help the children to share out the fruit. They would like to have half each.

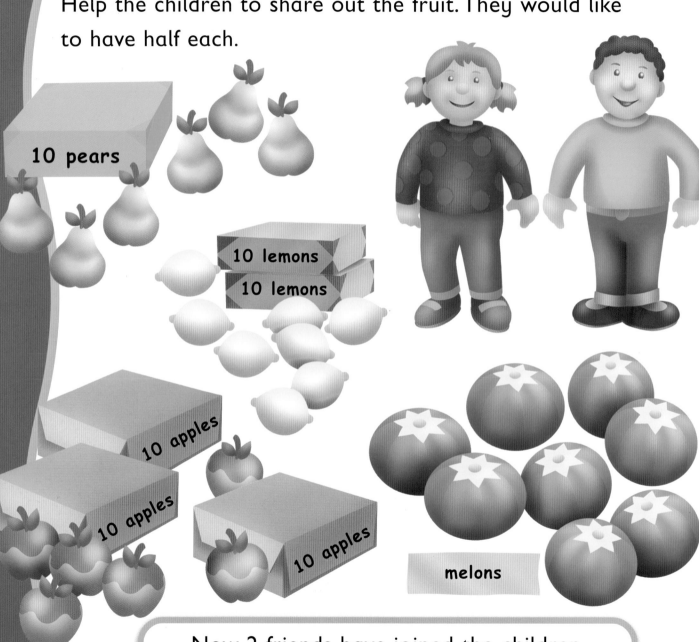

10 pears

10 lemons

10 lemons

10 apples

10 apples

10 apples

10 apples

melons

Now 2 friends have joined the children.
Give each child a quarter each of the fruit.

16

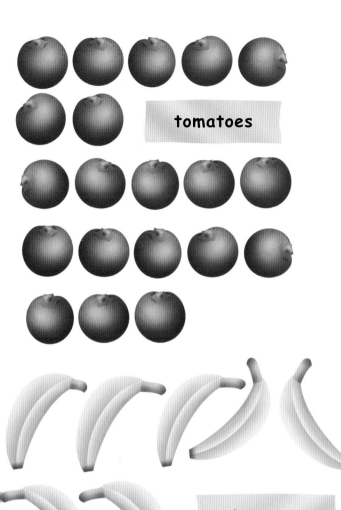

tomatoes

Now try this

You will need some squared paper and coloured pencils. Draw a rectangle. Colour half the squares blue. Draw different rectangles and colour half blue. Try colouring in different ways.

bananas

strawberries

10 oranges

10 oranges

17

Finding halves

All the numbers on the clowns' balloons are halves of the numbers on the elephants. Match each number on an elephant to its half on a clown's balloon.

Some of the elephant numbers can be divided into quarters. Can you find 2 of these?

9

90

Challenge

Which of these numbers can be quartered: 4, 14, 24, 34? Write down 5 more numbers that can be quartered.

$4 \div 4 =$

7

16

6

8

70

12

19

Fingers and thumbs

Some of the children in Mrs Jones' class counted their fingers and thumbs and discovered that there were 90 in total. How many children were there? If some children counted fingers, thumbs and toes and counted to 100, how many children is that?

Tell a friend how you worked out the answer.

Challenge

How many children are in your class at school? How many fingers and thumbs are there altogether? How many toes? So, how many digits (fingers, thumbs and toes) are there in total in your class?

Supporting notes

Equal grouping – pages 4–5

If the children are unsure about division by repeated subtraction, or grouping, provide some counters. Ask the children to count out the same quantity of counters as there are flowers, then to divide the counters between the vases equally. They can count each set of counters to check that each vase has the same quantity.

Equal sharing – pages 6–7

Children may begin to share by saying, 'one for you and one for me,' until they have shared all the items. Encourage them to think about the multiplication facts that they know. For example, if they know that 3x2=6, then 6 shared by 3 is 2.

Dividing by 2 – pages 8–9

Children should begin to derive the division facts for 2 from their knowledge of the 2 times-table. Say together the 2s multiplication table, then say the division table: 2 divided by 2 is 1; 4 divided by 2 is 2… If they are still unsure, then start with some counters.

Dividing by 10 – pages 10–11

If children struggle with division by 10, model it using counters. If necessary, point out that the digits move one place to the right, so that 20÷10 is 2. Use the strategy outlined above (*Dividing by 2*) of saying the 10s multiplication table, then the 10s division table: 10 divided by 10 is 1; 20 divided by 10 is 2…

Dividing by 3, 4 and 5 – pages 12–13

There are no visual clues to help with the division. If children find this difficult, they may like to use counters to share out. Alternatively, use a number line. For 12÷3, for example, count back in jumps of 3 from 12 to 0. Ask, 'How many jumps did we make? – so 12÷3 is 4.'

Finding remainders – pages 14–15

Children who need extra help with this activity could use counters to model the division and to find the remainder. Alternatively, use a number line and count back in equal jumps. For dividing 7 by 2, count back from 7 in 2s. The children will find that they will have a remainder of 1.

Halves and quarters – pages 16–17

This activity is designed to help children make the link between division and finding fractions of quantities. If they are unsure, suggest that they count out small even quantities of counters and to find half. When they are confident with this, count out quantities that can be divided by four, ask them to find half, then half again. Explain that this gives quarters.

Finding halves – pages 18–19

Where children know their 2 times-table, they should be able to find halves quickly, deriving the half fact from a multiple of 2. Some of these numbers are multiples of 10. If children are unsure about finding their halves, use a number line to find 0 and the decade number. Suggest that they look for the mid-point. Talk about how, where the decade digit is odd, half will have a 5 in the units, and where it is even, it will have 0 in the units.

Fingers and thumbs – pages 20–21

This activity involves dividing by 10 to find the number of children. However, when including toes, the children will need to think about dividing by 10 and by 2. If they are unsure about this, model it with real fingers, thumbs and toes.

Using this book

The illustrations in this book are bright, cheerful and colourful, and are designed to capture children's interest. Sit somewhere comfortable together, as you look at the book. Children of this age will normally be able to read most of the instructional words. Help with the reading where necessary, so that all children can take part in the activities, regardless of how fluent they are at reading at this point in time.

Children will find it useful to use their knowledge about multiplication when dividing. For example, if they know that 6x3=18, they can work out that 3x6=18, 18÷6=3 and 18÷3=6. These four facts are related, and any one of these that is known leads to the other three facts. In this book, children are shown division by grouping into equal sets and division by sharing into equal sets. Grouping can be seen as the same as repeated subtraction, so that 12÷3 can be found by repeatedly subtracting 3: 12-3=9; 9-3=6; 6-3=3; 3-3=0, so 4 amounts of 3 were subtracted and 12÷3=4. This can be modelled by repeated subtraction for a set of counters, or as repeated subtraction using a number line. Equal sharing can be seen as, 'One for you, one for me…' until everything is shared out, then the quantity for each person can be counted. Children are introduced to the concept of remainders, or what is left, after equal sharing or grouping.

Encourage the children to explain how they worked out the answers to the questions. Being able to explain their thinking, and to use mathematical vocabulary, helps the children to clarify in their mind what they have just done. Also, where there are children who are not so sure of how to solve the problem, hearing what others did, and how they did this, helps them to use these methods more effectively.

Do encourage children to make notes as they work at an activity. They can record numbers, writing them in order, or write simple sentences to explain. Encourage them to be systematic in the way that they work, so that they do not miss a vital part of the evidence that they need to find a solution.

Above all, enjoy together the mathematical games, activities and challenges in this book.